DREAMSCAPE VOYAGE

Dreamscape Voyage

poems by Alex Arnot

Haley's
Athol, Massachusetts

© 2022 by Alex Arnot.

All rights reserved. With the exception of short excerpts in a review or critical article, no part of this book may be re-produced by any means, including information storage and retrieval or photocopying equipment, without written permission of the publisher, Haley's.

Haley's
488 South Main Street
Athol, MA 01331
haley.antique@verizon.net • 978.249.9400

Copy edited by Richard Bruno.
Cover photo by Natalie Reynolds.

Library of Congress Cataloging-in-Publication Data
Names: Arnot, Alex, 1996- author.
Title: Dreamscape voyage / poems by Alex Arnot.
Description: Athol, Massachusetts : Haley's, [2022] | Summary: "This collection of poetry by Alex Arnot includes introspective considerations of personal experience with depression as well as short narrative poems with fantasy and horror themes"-- Provided by publisher.
Identifiers: LCCN 2022056229 (print) | LCCN 2022056230 (ebook) | ISBN 9781948380690 (paperback) | ISBN 9781948380720 (adobe pdf)
Subjects: LCGFT: Poetry.
Classification: LCC PS3601.R5858 D74 2022 (print) | LCC PS3601.R5858
(ebook) | DDC 813/.6--dc23/eng/20221128
LC record available at https://lccn.loc.gov/2022056229
LC ebook record available at https://lccn.loc.gov/2022056230

*Hold fast to dreams
For if dreams die
Life is a broken-winged bird
That cannot fly.*
—Langston Hughes

Contents

Personal/Nature

A Lovely Rain. 3
Lunar Lullaby. 4
Sunset 5
Fading Faces. 6
Into the River 7
My Winter Sheath 8
Oblivion 9
Parasitic Predator 10
Relinquish. 11
The Lotus 13
Thy Kingdom Come 14
Thy Will Be Done 15
My Strangest Dream 16
I Like the Rain 17
That Distant Figure 18
Withered. 19
Our Fantasies 20
Bogeyman. 21
Creeping Shadow. 22
Lament 23
To Be Nothing 25
Idol 26

Social Commentary/Political

Ashes 1 31
Ashes 2 32
Ashes 3 33
Last of Ashes 34

Johnny's Requiem...........................35
Bite Your Tongue..........................36
Ice......................................37
Monster and Child.........................38
No Time to Dream..........................39
There Is No Destiny.......................40
Digital Screen............................41
Your Soul is Mine.........................42
Curse of Nostalgia........................43
Fight!...................................44
Unnatural................................45
A Child's Dream..........................46

Fantasy

King of the Red Skies.....................51
Tyrant...................................52
The Beetle...............................53
The Conduit..............................54
My Lovely Specter........................56
The Reaper's Prayer......................57
Realm of Sleep...........................58

Dreamscape Voyage

Plains of Wonder.........................63
Sea of Fear..............................64
River of Sorrow..........................65
Clouds of Desire.........................66
Desert of Pride..........................67

Horror

Sleep....................................73
Creep....................................75
Mist Breather............................76
Illusions................................77
Postmortem Portrait......................79
Tale of a Solemn Tombstone...............80
Made for Me..............................81
Body Farm................................82

How it Feels to Lose Your Skin 84
Acknowledgements. 89
About the Poet 91
Colophon 95

Beginning Somewhere

a foreword by Candace R. Curran

Alex had me at ". . . writing through a struggle with depression, reflected in morbid and depressing poetry."

One must begin somewhere, and that's how it was for me at the same age, lying on the warm earth in the backyard looking skyward, heavy and unable to fly . . . wondering if I was going to make it and began, painfully, finding and pinning words to paper that would save me.

We can right ourselves, write ourselves out of places of circumstance and trauma, if we are lucky, and persevere. Depression is like that, and yes, journaling, capturing, documenting, creating save as words become dark lullabies, a catalyst for endurance and change. Alex, as I had, found a key for survival and thriving.

Let us visit, be entertained, find kinship in our shared monsters where self is sometimes vampire and poetry, the dagger.

Not all roses, Alex gives us in the beauty of lyrical hauntings his obsessive nightmares and his melancholy musings. In "I Like the Rain," he writes.

Yes, I like the rain.
Its melancholy matches my own.
Its steady rhythm puts me at ease.
And though I thought I missed the sun
After the winter overstayed its welcome,
truth is, I miss the rain
and all my darkness that it brings . . .

Here we have arrived with his mythic, ballad-like poems in that slippery place between reality and dream. Alex's voice, brave and authentic, cozies up with eulogy's otherworldly, fork-split tongue. Lose yourself in the theater. You are invited to read to escape, to discover the metered path laid bare in this sometimes sardonic, always authentic collection.

Candace R. Curran is the author of *Playing in Wrecks* and a co-author of the collaboration, *Bone Cages* (with John Hodgen, Doug Anderson, and others), both published by Haley's Press. Her poems have been published in *Meat For*

Tea, *Silkworm*, *RAWNerVZ*, and elsewhere; and anthologized in *Writing the Land, Honoring Nature, WTL: Northeast, Poet's Seat Poetry Silver Anniversary, Compass Roads*, and *Poems in the Time of Covid*. She has won the Poets Seat Contest twice. Candace has organized and participated in word and image collaborations including Four On The Floor, Three On a Tree, INTERFACE I-IO, and Exploded View. She has also served children and adults for many years in both public and school libraries. Candace's partner is a librarian, and books are an important part of their world.

Personal/Nature

A Lovely Rain

The summer's heat has calmed its rage.
A sky once blue has turned to grey.
Some say rain can kill one's mood,
   but I find peace within the dark—

   restful sleep on rainy nights,
   a steady pace on rainy days,
   pitter-patter on the window—
   the quiet symphony of the storm.

Lunar Lullaby

I am the one who calms the seas.
I am the eyes that see you sleep
   as you listen to the breeze
   making music with the leaves.

I smile at you in the night.
With the stars I set the sky alight
   to illuminate at my behest
   until the sunshine lets me rest.

Sunset

As crimson breaks through a cloudy sea,
sunshine bids its last adieu.
Vibrant flame through a fissure of fading azure
displays majesty before it's through.

Dull white clouds are painted pink,
and blackening skies are lulled to sleep
before the night does come awake:
in tranquil calm forever keep.

For life is burned into the world,
and in the flame is beauty incarnate.
Evening unleashes its masterpiece
as sky erupts in radiant scarlet.

Fading Faces

No longer dreaming, I'm wide awake.
With every sigh, it gets easier to take.
But I'm missing the answers that I seek
   and still the tears run down my cheek.

I remember fondly the happy days,
   but all the same it brings me pain.
Along the road, you lost your way—
   the only thing familiar is your face.

Who are you now, and could I ever know you?
Are you really gone? Could it be true?
If you'd only look me in the eye
   for one last time to say goodbye.

Into the River

In silence, I drifted along the river.
I never gave a thought to the surrounding shore.
There were mountains to climb up on dry land,
    but I felt life had run its course.

Nothing to hear but the river's hum,
The cold meant nothing as I lost all feeling—
    couldn't tell if I were still in motion.
That I was in the river is all that mattered.

I drowned inside the river.
Don't know if I made it out to sea.
But here I lie in rigor mortis,
    my mind soon to drift away with the stream.

My Winter Sheath

After winter, I can finally be at peace
    after I've shivered a hundred nights at least.
To quell the flame inside that eats away at me,
    to swallow down my rage and put my mind at ease,

    my thoughts once flowed like a gentle stream,
    but after the summer, they turned to a stormy sea

    building this lonesome shell I have been in so long.
Every time I inhaled, I breathed in a poison fog.
Anger and grief brought me to places I don't belong.
Thought I was justified, but know now I was wrong,

    pulled through by kindness I have been shown.
For so many nights, I have shivered here on my own.
I had snuffed out the summer in my winter sheath
    and entered the spring now finally relieved.

Calm are the waves, and the storm will subside.
Winter's almost over, and I'm still alive.

Enter the river: I can finally be at peace.
Now that it's over, I can lay me down to sleep,
    sweet serenity in my hands for me to keep,
    anger and grief cast way down into the deep.

Oblivion

A wasteland walked so many times:
    cling to a thought then cast it aside.
Mental pictures sway to and fro
    then drift into the undertow.

Indifferent to what once impressed,
    my mind neglects my previous interest.
Mental traditions I wished to hold,
    but new concerns outweigh the old.

I'm distracted by life's shapeless form.
No image I can call the norm.
The calm now rarely I recall—
Better I suppose than not at all.

Parasitic Predator

Insatiable hunger drives me to enter
   an exquisite insecurity, oh, so tender!
      aches and pains
      mentally drained
      dizzy and faint
      comfy and quaint

For me, your body is the perfect abode.
I live in luxury as your mind corrodes!
I expelled your charisma as I bored inside,
   tearing you apart, and still I hide.

A lack of focus:
   my magnum opus,
   for when you're drained,
   I remain—
   feel your heart sinking into your stomach!
Through your thoughts I gleefully rummage,
   searching your dread for things I can play with,
   for torturous toys used through the ages.

      weary flesh
      shortened breath
      jaded eyes
      unsatisfied

Relinquish

   Sad little creature,
     forlorn little beast,
alone you lie,
     solitary as you are.
Give up Give Up GIVE UP
Pain becomes you.
Hurt defines you.
So it is
     and forever shall be.
Join . . . NOW
Surrender . . . NOW
Relinquish . . . NOW
     the entirety of your being.

Your life is a sinking boat,
     a sick and twisted little joke.
Through ember, flame, and blinding smoke,
     your end my song does still evoke.

You broken child,
     you withered heart,
     so much ennui
     consumed by woe—

Come on Come On COME ON
My melody means to end your grief,
     a somber tune to end your sorrow,
     and with that knife you'll suffer no longer—
     one last note to bring relief.

Join . . . NOW

Surrender . . . NOW
Relinquish . . . NOW
   your worldly skin and weary mind.

The Lotus

Our garden grew so many things
    each with beauty all its own.
You planted your seeds, and I had mine,
    I wished for one we'd grow together.

We sat and pondered what we'd plant—
    so many choices, so little space.
To the end, we were divided.
I wanted a lotus, and you a tree.

We decided there was room for both,
    but bitterness still stained your heart.
You made me care for it on my own
    and hoarded supplies for your tree.

I got my lotus food and water.
I toiled away at my own pace.
You thought that your tree would bear you fruit
    and that I'd stare in awe and envy.

Over time, my lotus blossomed,
    and though it hadn't much to give,
    it never did me any harm,
    and I was proud of what I'd made.

THY KINGDOM COME

Oh, heal me now, great and knowledgeable one,
    for empty I am until thy kingdom come.
Oh, build a paradise just for me
    and assure that I am truly free.

So long I've spent building myself,
    but you claim I'm still a broken shell.
So blunt the statement, it must be truth.
The person made must be removed.

So, burn thy will into my mind
    until I'm truly lost and blind.
My soul is gone, and here I dwell—
    a paradise now that once was Hell.

THY WILL BE DONE

Heathen scum
    I am forevermore, my faith undone.
Further I drift from the prodigal son.
Damned be I who abstains from the one—

Heretic slime,
    the unholiest sins that blind my eyes.
Fuck your will-restraining lies
    and seething words that stained my mind,

Infidel worm
    my soul to take, my soul to burn,
    rend my flesh and watch me squirm.
Claim to teach but never learn.

Godless knave,
    the tainted blood that rolls like waves
    undulating through my veins,
    try to save me while you pray.

My Strangest Dream

A most peculiar set of events unfolded
   in the darkness where my dreams are molded.
With the warmest smile on her face,
   she found me in my favorite mental haze,
   gave the key to find her once more.
"Reach out for me," she did implore.

Before the dream began to fade
   as I begged my mind to let me stay
   tightly gripping that world of fiction—
"It's more than fantasy" was my conviction—
   one last thing I had to save,
   the final piece. It was her name.

And so, the morning greeted my eyes.
My conscious mind then came alive.
After the morning's toil ceased,
   I'd set out to decode my dream.
On social media, I searched your name,
   and to my surprise I found your face.

I've never believed in destiny,
   but how could I possibly explain what I've seen?
It never really amounted to anything,
   such a coincidental happening,
   though surely it has to have some meaning,
   for a mind can't dream a face from nothing.

I Like the Rain

This won't be metaphorically spoken,
for I'm not in the mood to spin and weave my words as such.
Stress and rage have taken their toll for the day,
and the cooling rain has gone away.

Yes, I like the rain.

Its melancholy matches my own.
Its steady rhythm puts me at ease.
And though I thought I missed the sun
After the winter overstayed its welcome,

truth is, I miss the rain

and all my darkness that it brings to the surface
of all the angry and somber song lyrics,
all the dreary stories I love to read.
Because joy is not the only emotion.

And as such, I want the rain

to wash away the burning daylight,
to sooth my soul the way no other weather can,
to play a tune that mutes the bullshit,
to remind me the world can weep as well.

THAT DISTANT FIGURE

Out of body and given wholly to mind,
   a nexus for life and time to bind—
   again, that distant figure walks away.

So many times,
   yes, so many I've given chase
   only so that it may increase its haste.

But now my being here I lay.
I stay until it finally fades—
   gone,
   and I'll pursue no more.

Was I ever meant to catch it?
Who knows?
Yet still that figure comes and goes.

Neither looking nor speaking,
   it invites me not,
   and I've cast it entirely out of thought.
Or so I say.

Tediously marching in endless space,
   it once seemed to have a familiar face,
   though the eyes were always blank and empty.

Why then do I still wonder
   where it may lead me if I follow,
   that silent figure with eyes so hollow?

Withered

A mighty stone that once was proud
    now lies withered on the ground.
Day by day it chipped away,
    until its shell began to fade.

Supporting the weight of weaker gravel
    that turned to rock as the stone unraveled,
    the way that time has shaped this land
    has made this stone turn into sand.

The newer rocks will try to carry
    mighty stone that's weak and weary,
    and when the stone has finally shattered,
    memories will live in the sand that's scattered.

Our Fantasies

Lost within your own little world,
    you and reality don't get along.
The things you say transcend all logic—
    lyrics of a mad man's song
    and still, somehow, I understand it, too.

My own perceptions contradict sanity.
I'm caught up in such attractive illusions.
I perceive truth, based on my own experience,
    different colors of the same delusions,
    falsified pictures of life untrue.

So perhaps you and I aren't so different,
    both hidden from the real world's icy fingers.
Our shared pains blanketed by unique filters,
    the thought's ignored yet still it lingers,
    bound to whatever belief you choose.

Though this vision of yours I'll never share,
    never know what lives in your sight.
But in your fantasy, you're not alone
    nor in your joy nor in your strife.
Perhaps reality was meant to be skewed.

Bogeyman

Moonlight offers sympathy
   as I stare at an empty street tonight.
Are you held up by your drunken state
   or the poison flowing through your veins?

The more I wait, the worse I fear
   until at last, your shape appears

   as I watch you stumble home in the dark
   in a toxic haze that numbs your pain.
So afraid
   to tell me what does haunt your mind,
   and so, a sad scene plagues my eyes.
Until you finally face the truth,
   your bogeyman still waits for you.
A somber veil he watches through.

Until sober and stable you can keep,
   your nightmares will not ever cease.
In your darkest dreams, I wish you peace.

Creeping Shadow

I watch the people walk along
Alone
Alone
Kindred, more with the dark that follows.

Hiding
Gone
   from a vibrant world that feels so wrong
Private
Lonesome
Longing to consume what I can't swallow.

To the shadow, back I slither,
   reaching for that which burns my skin.
Here inside the dark I wither
with my own folly once again.

Where oblivion calls me back to rest
   in broken sleep, my dreams distress.
In shackles of my own design,
I lose the key and stay confined.

Somewhere far beyond this cage,
   the darkness holding me shall fade.

Distant dreams
Finally free
Someday soon
   no more gloom?

Lament

God has gone away,
    and even the holiest saint won't pray
    for me.
Jesus Christ has lost his patience.

Did well in school,
    but only in the dead eyes of machines—
    a thread of twine in a ribbon of lies,
    a streak of polish on a shiny trophy.

My best friend went away,
    locked up in his world of lonesome.
The one who helped me find myself
    fell quiet and then disappeared—
    took a fragment of my heart
    and gave shape to what I so long feared,
    a friendship consumed by bitter silence.

My sweet cat passed away.
The pain, the tears, the dreams won't fade.
Still haunted by your precious face
    with me since I was a child,
    I never got to say goodbye.
Your departure split my heart in two.
In solitude still, I long to hold you.

Suppressing only goes so far.
Every day, the drink is tempting,

    to be lulled into a deathlike sleep
    bestowed upon me by the kiss of whiskey.
The world around distorts and fades,
    falling away.
My consciousness is slipping,
    for hours to be cradled in toxic bliss.
For hours, did I really live?
Who can say?
Though I'd have spared myself some pain,
    and I guess that'd be enough to say I'm living.

For now I sit inside my cage.
Near to me, the dark shall fade.

    No more dreams
    Finally free
    Someday soon
    No more gloom

To Be Nothing

For what do you want to be remembered?
What legacy do you want to leave behind?

Maybe I want to be nothing
    but a shadow gliding on the ground,
    no mark to leave but a pleasant memory,
    no mention of my name left to abound.

Still, I know it's unrealistic.
My words before you contradict.
    I'm fine to share my thoughts with you
    whose expectations don't constrict

    these words taken to heart only in death.
Maybe that's the way it's meant to be.
When life demands your presence no more,
    what you've made is what is seen.

Forgotten all, my body lies
    in the dirt with my own ink,
    cocooned in pages of my own words
    that in my own thoughts forever sink.

Idol

White-fleeced fools who've gone astray,
    fulfill your bleak and empty lives.
I remedy now your wasted time.
At last, your new god has arrived.

Propitiate with fervor great.
Bestow gratuity unto me.
Like doctrine, you will harken so.
Take my virtue as your creed.

Have you had lonely days for far too long?
Do you count ad nauseam nigh eternally?
Need not the sun. I ignite your screen.
No need for friends, but only me!

Daily, my sermon medicates your mind.
You wait hours for a moment of joy.
Just when reason begs you to think twice,
    here I have your medicine, boy!

So it is. I've made my fortune.
I leave you cold, alone, and sick.
You're not my problem anymore.
Cling to another to get your fix!

Social Commentary/Political

Ashes 1

Commence with your plight of devastation.
Ravenous eyes command eager hands to pull the trigger.
The victims' faces reflect your anger,
   then turn to despair before they fade—
   a premonition of what's to come
   buried deep beneath the ashes.

Segregation leads to death
   as the united plan retaliation
   and the chance to extend or reach a helping hand
   relinquished for your petty pride.
The evolution of humankind
   shall burn away to bitter ashes.

We choose to be American, European, Asian,
   and deny the fact that we're all human.
We unite only in times of crisis
   but only with those who share our feelings
   as those who challenge the madness are cast away
   alone to walk upon the ashes.

Ashes 2

Are you sleeping in the dust
   or do you lie amongst the rust?
I was nineteen when I died
   before the mess, no time to cry.

My fate was sealed with one cruel twist
   when they bestowed the bullet's kiss
   between the eyes, all turned to grey.
Beneath the mud, my corpse decays.

Here in Limbo, I remain
   to look upon the world in flames,
   archaic race all laid to waste,
   forsaken life, now empty space.

Ashes 3

Lying together on crimson sand
   filled with holes by anxious hands,
   surrounded by friends, yet he's still alone.
Weary legs now carry him home.

A thousand horrors overcome,
   but his people say the work is not done.
He sees them frothing at the teeth
   when they say awaken, but he's not asleep.

Ripping, tearing, they claw his heart
   until it's sufficiently torn apart.
The game is set for one last turn
   to ignite the world and let it burn.

Last of Ashes
Here is where we crossed the line,
   and just as well, I'd have to say.
We've fucked ourselves in every way.

Out of chances.
Out of time.
The time we've squandered now has died,
   a tragic death that none shall mourn.
Alone in Limbo, I sit forlorn,

   waiting until the end begins—
   no absolution for our sins,
   a path of burning ruin made.
Its toxic death does suffocate.

Architects of our own demise,
   one way or another, I surmise
   humankind shall fade away,
   a heavy debt with Hell to pay.
Here inside my shell, I stay
   as the world around falls to decay—

   deaf to the cries of mortal coil,
   the lungs that fill with sludge and oil,
   skin that burns in nuclear waste,
   smell of blood so strong I taste.
Dying lie in searing rain,
   one final shot that ends their pain—

   gone, with only dust to stay.

Johnny's Requiem

You did so love the summer days,
    the warm wind blowing on your face
    finding bliss in a loved one's gaze,
    soft sand, and ocean waves.
But you were sent off to your grave.
That "honor" that did seal your fate.

Now Johnny lies beneath the roses,
    his casket buried in the rain
By callous hands, his life was stolen.
He gave his body and lost his name,

    nevermore to feel life's joys,
    denied your love to die a drone
    to raise your gun beside the big boys,
    to fall together yet die alone.

Now your dreams are thrown away,
Whichever god, your soul do take.
Forever neath the ground to stay,
    a thousand more shall go and fade,
The youth whose lives were never made,
    the youth that only got a taste.

The nameless lie beneath the roses,
    their caskets buried in the rain.
By callous hands, their lives were stolen—
    gave their bodies and lost their names.

Bite Your Tongue

You curse my name from inside your cage
   with restrictive bars that your allies made.
So eager you are to share your chains,
   though in time these locks will become your bane.

To provide me a cell or sever my tongue,
   enslave the old and condition the young.
For thoughtful minds to be veiled by silence,
   cantankerous words give way to violence.

Sway me

   with a challenging thought, with which I cannot argue,
   not with terms that question my virtue.
Change my mind with clever wit.
Never turn your head and spit,

   for if the burden of this prison be too great,
   the mettle of others; hearts you slate
   may freeze their shoulders when help you seek
   or deny their kindness when havoc wreaks.

Ice

Step on me, and I can break you.
As I shatter, I can cut you.

Prolonged exposure to me will harden you.
The colder I get, the denser I become.

But give me warmth, and I can cool you.
As I lose mass, I can ease your pain.

When I flow free, I can sustain your life.
The warmer I get, the more I can give you.

Monster and Child

I curse your flesh,
    and I curse your bones.
I loathe the blood that makes you whole.
I hate you to your very soul.

I see the anger, fear, and grief
    as your teary eyes look back at me.
Every night I cannot sleep,
    another day I'll make you scream.

Another strike across your face
    means quick escape from my disgrace.
It's over now. You're on the ground,
    I call, but you don't make a sound.

I carried you within my womb.
Now I lay you in your tomb.
My blood leaked from your veins,
    my flesh buried under your grave.

No Time to Dream

Sleep what's needed and dream no more—
    only enough for your energy restored.
May we keep you anxious of what's to come
    and ever more, your mind goes numb.

Inspired no longer by souls exposed,
    desire to create has decomposed.
Emptied your mind of wind and rain—
    kept you bound by iron chains.

Now smile pretty and prepare to see
    this vile prison we've made for thee.
Here you'll stay confined forever
    or at least until your will is severed.

THERE IS NO DESTINY

You tell me that by some force I'm driven,
    but I feel no pull and see no strings.
I paint my path with my own choices
    even when others give me colors.

You can try to work with the hand you're given,
    but the hand of fate can always be discarded.
The die can roll on six sides only,
    but more dice can always be added.

Some say life is not a game,
    but they keep trying so hard to win.
They then tell others they can never
    so that they'll kick the chair and forfeit.

Digital Screen

"Your clothes are lame.
Your dance is gay.
Don't know you, but I don't like your face.

"Keep doing what you love to do,
and I will hide and laugh at you
from these digital eyes I see life through."

When did the world become so toxic?
Why are people so obnoxious?
This digital screen you hide behind
   where all you do is criticize
   every aspect of everyone else's lives
   while you sit still as the sands of time
   waste away and pass you by.

"My thoughts are my words.
And my word is law.
The law decrees that you suck shit through a straw.

"What's the matter, don't like what I say?
You'll never find me anyway.
The digital screen will hide my face.
The digital screen will keep me safe."

Your Soul is Mine

Surrender your life to me.

In industrial shackles eternally bound,
    a hole where the moribund spirit lies
    empty, like the promise of better days,
    the soul decays and putrefies.

Fatigue oxidizes the chains
    that dig into your gangrenous flesh:
    fetid bones and dying ghost,
    surrounding stench of lingering death.

Surrender your time to me,

    time that marches on and on,
    a ballad of monotony for marching pawns.
Slaves to avarice's wretched spawn.
Pay tribute to freedom's perfect con!
And now that your life and time are gone . . .

Surrender your soul to me.

Your very essence to me relinquished,
    an enthusiastic light extinguished,
    to this ancient order soon succumb,
    determination now undone,
    a new creed to which you will abide.
Your life, your time, your soul is mine.

Curse of Nostalgia
I don't want it anymore.

I can feel life's judging eyes glare at me.
Upon me, the sun no longer smiles.
Flirtatious media calls "stay awhile."
Only a glimpse of others' lives,
   an emptiness does satisfy.

New voices have tainted my escape.
My apathy threatened by their pain,

   I don't want it anymore.

Oh, sweet teat of nostalgic things!
Cradled, I suckle, and you sweetly sing.
Bury me gently in familiar bliss.
Shelter me now and save me from this

   pain
   swallowed down by sweet nostalgia,
   pain
   inflicted by the real world's careless fingers.

Doped up by memories of the past
   when hope did promise the joy would last,
   eyes, perhaps, not tainted by rose
   but blind to misfortune not my own
   tell me a story I know so well
   free of the pandering they try to sell.

Upon me, the screen no longer smiles.
Only memories let me stay awhile,
   and I don't want it anymore.

FIGHT!
It's not a battle I incite.
I question why you need to fight?
Does joining a cause make you feel fulfilled?
When completed, will you be sated still?
What reason to live when the fight is gone?
What demon will you make of the next who breathes wrong?
Is it thrill or purpose in your blood?
What thoughts for those dragged through the mud,
    public relations forever strained,
    no reconciling honor that's been stained.

Consume bile spewed from shady sources.
Armed with keys, gain brainwashed forces.
Their lies that robbed you of your sleep
    induct you into an army of sheep,
    bleating legions marching on—
    a one-track mind that's going strong.

Welcome to the family, never stray,
    for if thoughts arise you might betray,
    a thousand lies will stoke their fear.
Once allied mouths, your name shall smear.

Unnatural

No more use for a weary brain.
No defiance of nature, now its slave.
I need it simple and black and white.
I need an endless war to fight.

I'm tired,

    tired of questioning everything,
    struggling with turmoil, burning within.

You're unnatural.

It's easier to think of you this way.
In perfect order, my mind won't stray.

"I'm scared,

    scared to consider I might be misguided,
    unnatural, sub-human. It's been decided."
This, the mirror chants back to me,
    and I don't like the man I see.

Something about him is . . . unnatural.

A Child's Dream

In sleep last night, my dreams did yield
   of a small boy sat in a windy field.
I asked him why he was alone,
   was shocked to find his face was my own.
I was taken aback by what he said:
"I'm scared of the pictures in my head!"
Confused, I asked him to set the scene.
"Tell me, my child, what you see!"

"I see haunted schools where no one talks,
   where bullet-ridden corpses walk;
   red-eyed men with pulsing veins
   drive swerving cars all smeared with brains.
No alabaster cities gleam—
   just empty buildings and broken dreams,
   faceless zombies holding screens,
   smoggy skies and filthy streams.
Perverted gazes stare at me
   then stand upon their pegs and preach.
I see humans hooked up to machines
   that are run by the shadowy hands of greed.
This, good sir, is what I see
   when I lay me down to sleep."

Fantasy

King of the Red Skies

Lacerated skin so dry and grey,
    blood-soaked hair on my head and face,
    skeleton wings with scarlet flames,
    silver claws that tear and maim—

    been burning here for years with rage,
    been screaming for you to correct that mistake,
    been listening carefully to all that you say,
    been aching to rip the bars from my cage,

    been waiting to bring the evil I crave,
    been counting down the nights and days.
The morals of man have withered me away,
    but they'll never kill me. I remain.

Tyrant

Because I breathe,
   you owe me everything.
Unless you're me,
   you deserve nothing.
Live in my shadow
   or be crushed beneath my feet.

Either way, you're still a bug.
You cannot live without my permission.
And even when you become me,
   all you'll receive is scraps.
Anything more might make you stronger,
   and I must keep you far below me.

I sit here on my throne of skulls,
   watching over all the worms.
A nightcrawler rises from its filth
   and bores itself into my heart.
As I die, a thought still haunts me:
   the worms will feast upon my carcass.

The Beetle

The sweetest song comes when the stars abound
    and the insects of the kingdom anticipate the sound.
A violinist beetle plays through the night
    when his firefly cousins deliver their light.

He sits on a dew-soaked stem alone.
Beneath the moonlight, it becomes his throne.
He plays a tune that would make songbirds cry
    and creates new life under the darkened sky.

His music bids the other beetles sing along,
    and moths and spiders work in sync with his song.
Upon his stem, his heart writes symphonies sublime,
    some dark as the sky above, others like the stars that shine.

The Conduit

For he, indeed, a comatose shell became.
Now heed this story I relay
    as I regale you with the tale of woe.
You will, a dismal secret know.

Mankind was once at one with darkness.
A wicked, monstrous power harnessed
    and into its skin, the fleshlings slipped.
Their minds slowly into fragments ripped.

The weaker morsels swallowed down,
    the body consumed, the soul to drown.
The vile creatures from hate did spawn.
The infection to grief and spite respond.

The gods of old would soon decree
    a safeguard be placed to end the siege.
And of one pure child, the burden to bear,
    the folly of all mankind be shared.

And when the boy grew to a man,
   pain incarnate in his hands,
   years of bitter disdain and lies
   would bring the rage to fill his eyes.

The gods would then decide his fate,
   their fear that the evil will overtake
   shall bind him forever within his mind.
Warmth and joy he'll never find.

He eternally on his shackles feeds,
   the cruelest of all ironies.
A warning from this story true:
Darkness gives power absolute.

For should he awaken, the dark shall rise
   to take revenge on a world despised.
From the wretched masses, his army formed
   to again bring forth the abysmal storm.

My Lovely Specter

This is not how your story should end,
   but life ain't always a fairy tale, kid,
   and you did suffer every day
   for a false promise that the pain would go away.

You lie alone beneath a grave,
   epitaph chiseled beneath your name.
The hands of Limbo claimed your soul.
Your life was sold so long ago.

A friend in life, and you haunt me still
   for within my mind, you impose your will.
As I'm pulled into your darkest dream,
   helpless, I watch you cry and bleed.

He gave you up for a night with a whore.
He lost your love and so much more.
And when confronted, he lost his mind
   —his mind and body with rage gone blind.

As his fearful words painted your mood blue,
   his fatal grip changed your skin's hue.
Now that I've learned how your life ceased,
I hope I can help you rest in peace.

The Reaper's Prayer

I am he who governs death,
    for when thou takest thy final breath,
    my shadow rises at thy feet
    thy weak and weary soul to greet.
Abandon thy grief and worldly strife.
I free thy spirit and keep thy life.
In sorrow, thy eulogy is read aloud
    before thy body is lowered down.
The mourning lay thy frigid bones
    into the Earth, thy body sown.
Fear not my sickle nor blackened cloak,
    for I shall not torment thy ghost.
Thy next life beyond this world doth dwell,
    and requiem bids thy spirit farewell.

Realm of Sleep

Welcome to the Realm of Sleep,
    where a blissful lonesome waits for thee.
Thy former existence from whence thou fell
    hath bid thee here forever dwell.
Thy soiled flesh my aura cleanse,
    and to thy cell my will doth send.
Caught within these eyes of gold,
    thy limp frame by my breast I hold.
Here thy soul will eternally stay
    cradled. Thou lookest on my face.
Under starlight where my red locks gleam,
    in whisper, I bid thee sweetest dreams.
Beneath this cosmic sea I lay
    thy spirit within a grassy cave.
Until infinity passes by,
    in the Realm of Sleep thou now reside.

Dreamscape Voyage

PLAINS OF WONDER

Fatigued, my body prepares to sleep.
My eyelids close to fall in deep
    to this portal that brings me to my dreams
    and awakens my mind to an amazing scene—

    a vast moonlit plain before me,
    a gentle wind enhances its glory.
And then approaches a familiar stranger
I see no threat and feel no danger.

It's an ever-changing face forged from ones I'd known,
    and upon our locking eyes, their excitement had shown.
"You long for this world, so step inside.
You know my faces. I'll be your guide."

So began our journey there.
For once in my life, I was truly prepared
    to see the world my mind had made,
    to journey through what hides from day.

We wandered for what seemed like hours
    as that mighty field did boast its powers.
"Take a final look, and dry your tears,
    for next we sail the sea of fears."

SEA OF FEAR

They lead me to a two-man raft
   with the bottom made entirely of glass.
I asked them why the floor was transparent.
Why bring more strife to a sea so errant?

"The sea of fears shall test the brave.
You must overcome to calm the waves."
It became clear that it was no simple jaunt.
It would be on that path my fears would haunt.

As darkened waters tossed and turned,
   soon my anxiety began to burn,
   and to my horror, it took its form:
   a lurking beast within the storm.

"Two more forms must still appear—
   anxiety to paranoia and paranoia to fear."
And as my guide said, it transformed once more
   with features more terrifying than before.

Then fangs and scales met with spikes and horns,
   and with that, fear had taken form.
Its eyes reflected my real-life terrors,
   what I feared would come from all my errors.

"That's quite the monster, but what do you notice?"
Strange as it seemed it never approached us!
"Your fears can't harm you if you don't bait them to follow.
And now we approach the river of sorrow."

River of Sorrow

Into the river, our raft had veered.
As I looked over my shoulder, my guide disappeared.
I frantically searched and begged their return
Their voice spelled out my next lesson to learn.

"My faces are those you've seen in life,
    and though familiar, they bring you strife."
I realized I mustn't look but listen.
Verbal instruction would lead the mission.

Pitiful cries polluted the air.
Though I closed my eyes, I could feel them stare.
Remembering words and solemn pictures,
    forgotten psalms and empty scriptures,

I recognized voices of the dead
And tearful last words I have said.
Grief and sorrow held me in their sway.
Speaking to my guide did numb the pain.

"Often in life, a path can't be shown.
Only communication will make it known.
I shall return when the terrain grows higher.
Together we'll cross the clouds of desire."

CLOUDS OF DESIRE

Like magic, I ascended the mountain peak.
I'd hoped before, my guide would speak.
The next best thing to it, I suppose,
    they met me in person where the mountain rose.

With a gesture of hand, they bid me to see
    a vast sea of clouds stretching on perpetually.
A solitary bridge broke the consistent roll.
"Though it requires no currency, there is still a toll."

At long last, my guide's voice had resurged.
"To cross, you must resist temptation and avoid any urge!"
In only moments, I understood what they meant.
Visions my greatest desires had sent.

One by one, smoky images called out to me
    of lives I wanted and loves not meant to be.
"Should you fall, this dream will end.
You've come so far, why start over again?"

Advice from my guide returned my sense,
    and I knew to keep moving before the next wave commenced.
My guide never judged me for what they saw
    or any embarrassments that came from the maw.

"We all have hidden desires that no one should see.
Not letting them control you seems strength enough to me.
The end is in sight and our destination resides.
For now, we enter the forest of pride."

Desert of Pride

Finally, we reached the bridge's end
    the last of this world's enigmas to comprehend.
My guide's ever-changing face wore a disappointed stare.
I felt another lesson was about to be shared.

"Before us stretches an everlasting sand
    when in its place a mighty forest should stand.
Are you not proud of what you've made?
Has no joy you've experienced ever stayed?"

There was a time when a forest mighty may be
But doubt, fear, and angst has caused its decease.
Many a day I feel as though I walk this desert,
    miles of nothingness until my mood reverts.

"It would seem you've been to this place before,
    but now I am here to help you restore
    the canopy of trees razed by your pride.
Think long and hard. Reach deep inside"

I then began to ponder my life
    for anything positive to outshine the strife,
    and soon the memories overcame me.
Each pleasant thought slowly changed the scene.

For every realization, the ground did shift.
Leaves and sprouts from the sand did lift,
    replaced it with mud, then a grassy plain.
Further thought created a quenching rain.

"Though only saplings, in time they will grow.
Seek help, and eventually a forest you will know.
This world has nothing more to see.
For now, your journey is complete."

My dream then began to fade
   as I awoke to the rising light of day,
   lessons I learned still on my mind.
I will find right moments in life these lessons to apply.

Horror

Sleep

You've escaped me in life,
    and I don't like to be cheated.
The greatest way to cause you strife:
You won't rest unless you have a death-wish!

Turn on every machine,
    make yourself high on caffeine.

You only have time
    to say goodbye
    before your soul is mine.

Alone in the dark
    with your world falling apart,
    your mind unravels at the seams.
Fatigued, you fall into this dream
    coming ever closer here to me
    as you're falling asleep.
You've awakened once more,
    but, not for long.
Balance falters and vision distorts.

As you're blinking,
    the room is shrinking.

Your debt is due,
    and I'm collecting soon.
Before the dawn, I'll come for you!

Will you sleep,
    if Death wants you?
You won't dream,
    because I haunt you!

Surrender your life
    to ease your mind
Give in, lay down, and die.

Alone in the dark
    with the beating of your heart,
    it seems you can't escape from fate.
In this mindscape, here I wait.
Oddly relaxed and at peace,
    you're falling asleep.

Creep

I've been chasing you for so long,
    and you have nowhere left to hide.
In the darkness, I creep along.
Terror overwhelms your sight.

The wind howls at you a morbid song,
    an omen of what is to come.
This place familiar now feels so wrong
    as sanity becomes undone.
The moonlight scowls at you through the fog
    in the shadow of dying woodland greens.
Footsteps follow you through the bog.
You're taunted by twisted trees.

Dancing shadows congregate on the wall
    to distract you as I slither in.
As you take a gander at winding halls,
    the knife slips into your skin.

Mist Breather

Here your soul is mine to own.
Fate condemned you to wander Limbo
    forever under my domain,
    my dominion, and my reign.
Meander through empty, ashen plains.
Meander through forests stained in grey.

Your heart has stilled, devoid of feeling—
    twisted, bled and wrung of being.
Governed by a perpetual sense of confusion,
    afterlife's promise and disillusion.
Between Oblivion that calls your name
    and Paradise lost, is where you stay.

Echoes of mislaid voices never ending—
    cries for answers ever pending:
    here your hopes and dreams are robbed.
Your only companion is the fog.
And here o'er you, I watch with glee
    as you must now face eternity.

Illusions

Welcome to the house of mirrors.
Take a look around.
Look at all the funny faces—
    warping smiles, twisting frowns.
See yourself in many shapes there
    as you laugh and cry,
        distracted by obscene reflections
        and ignore what they hide.

Illusions
    all around you—
        they can see

Illusions—
    they surround you
    and disguise the freak.

Walking through a maze of glass,
    you swear you hear them speak.
Distorted voices reveal your secrets.
You question what you believe,
    things that only you could know
    and keep buried deep within—
    every dark, subconscious thought.
Every little sin.

The nightmare only getting worse,
    you start to lose your mind.

One lets out a horrid scream, jumps out
    and pulls you right inside.
Illusions
    all around you—
    they can breathe.

Illusions—
    they have found you.
You reside with freaks.

Postmortem Portrait

A pale cadaver that I see, cold and limp before my feet—
   a perfect portrait of the obscene,
   but here and now it brings intrigue.
Death like a perfect Broadway play
   lost yourself in such a way.
I've been tempted so many times to slay,
   but only now has come that day.
Skin and bone without a soul,
   possibilities fade as you turn cold.
Stiffening limbs and rotting flesh—
   my art that truly took your breath.
Now I put you on display
   in this museum that became your grave.
In the chair I sit with pride, satisfaction in my eyes
   despite the fate that waits for me—
   the price of creating my masterpiece.

Tale of a Solemn Tombstone

Name and advent carved in stone.
Dust and bone six feet below.
Decaying lungs of air bereft,
And writhing worms consume thy flesh.

A deity willed thy life expire,
for heinous sin evoked his ire.
'Neath murky deep of fear's great lake shall death await,
    thy soul to take,
    thy heart engorged in encroaching gloom
    and lurking presence of impending doom,

    thy deed of life owed to the dead,
    final anguish the wicked dread.
Tantalize the mouth of Hell,
    the sea of flame where monsters dwell.
The Devil lives behind their eyes,
    and demons mock tormented cries.
Woe of the damned and unholy glee
    now prepares a place for thee.

By Reaper's hand, thy book is closed.
Through trembling lips thy story told.
'Neath mangled branch of barren tree
    lies solemn tombstone:
Rest in Peace.

Made for Me

Here on this table before me lies
    a beautiful doll with shining eyes
    so perfect, so radiant, and so unique
    as if you were only made for me.
I hold you close. I understand
    what you should be is in my hands.

In time, your perfection begins to dim.
I lay you down and start again.
To remain how you are is what you want.
Protest not, Doll! You're mine to vaunt.
Forgive my temper. I mean not to speak ill.
Comply this once. I love you still.

But of course, once is never enough.
The road to perfection is always rough.
Again, I take you in my embrace,
    but no tenderness emanates from your face.
Grown cold to my touch—oh, tell me why!
You're made for me. You're meant to be mine!

Upon the table, I'll soon restore
    a smile sewn. You'll frown nevermore.
With rusty scissors, I'll cut your hair.
I tear your clothes. You're bald and bare.
With my thumb, I gouge your eye.
You're made for me. You're only mine!

Body Farm

Let it not be said that this wasn't expected.
I knew my choices would lead me here.
I lie in agony, rank and infested,
   waiting in misery to disappear.

My story begins in a city of crime.
When night fell, nobody could ever walk safe.
Scum of all kinds threatened innocent lives,
   and I was a crook just making my way.

Money and valuables—all was taken.
Ending a life never crossed my mind.
One bad decision left two men forsaken.
One tried to defend and had to die.

Trembling hands showed him unprepared.
Taking advantage, I pulled the trigger.
My heart skipped a beat when those sirens blared.
It seemed my problems had gotten bigger.

There I stood with my back to the wall.
Against the cops, I'd stand my ground.
No surrender, no punishment, only to fall.
I heard the shot that took me down.

I awoke in a weird, space-like dimension.
I feared no god, but boy, was I wrong.
A red-eyed celestial denied my ascension—
    told me in Hell is where I belong.

I pathetically tried to weasel a way out.
It said on earth, I could choose to stay.
My heart nearly burst when it told me about
    how I'd lie in my corpse 'til it rots away.

Donated to a farm for study,
    readied for decomposition to begin,
    placed in my cadaver, shot up and bloody,
    I see, I hear—I feel everything.

Covered only in a metal cage,
    I can taste the flies crawl down my throat.
Disgusted by the funk of my own decay,
    after four days' time, I start to bloat.

That's the story of my disgrace.
I can't wait until I'm finally dust,
    free of fluid leaking from my face and
    dread and maggots inside my guts.

How it Feels to Lose Your Skin

I was sentenced to death for falsified sin.
By wicked king's will they flay my skin.
Bound by quivering limbs speckled in beads of sweat,
    in unyielding horror, I await agonized death.
For hours, I hang in silent woe.
By what manner of depravity does he stoop so low?

Waiting . . .
Waiting . . .
The decaying of time exacerbates my torment.
Waiting . . .
Waiting . . .
Insurmountable fear makes me want to vomit.

The door bursts open as my tormentors come
    with malicious glee for the deed to be done.
Insanity takes me when they scrape their knives,
    sharpening and weaving them before my eyes.
Fear turns to dread inside my gut,
    and before too long they begin to cut,
    stripping away my skin from flesh.
Through taunts, I smell their putrid breath.
Exposed tissue spews crimson streams.
I've nearly gone deaf from my own screams.
Epidermis in slabs is peeled away—
    feels like I'm burning in an open flame.
Even my tears sting as I whimper and cry.
Don't know how long it took to die.
Dead.

Lying in darkness tranquil and calm,
   floating,
   savoring the moment as my pain is gone—
   empty,
   disappointed by how I was undone—
   angry—
   every part of my body calls for blood.

I awaken adrift on the Astral plane.
Nine cosmic entities hold me in their gaze.
A reflection of space composes their being.
Their stare contains a red star's gleam.
In still anticipation, they seem to wait.
In hurt and rancor, I begin to beg.
"I will forsake Paradise and Heaven's send
   if only you should grant me my revenge!"
With one final nod, they send me back.
The tyrants soon shall feel my wrath.

The two who flayed me shall be first.
Through death, I'll quench their sadistic thirst.
Still laughing at their masterpiece,
   my skinless corpse begins to breathe.
The celestials gave me inhuman strength.
With a furious scream, I break my chains.
In disbelief, their stares protest
   as I wrap my hands around their necks.
A fiery portal 'neath their feet
   opens as I start to squeeze.
With their final breaths, they've surely learned
   fear as I send their souls to burn.
And now the king shall meet his doom,
   his vile flesh by flies consumed.
Sitting on his undeserved throne,
   his life shall soon be mine to own.

Pounding, scratching on the wall,
    into the room I slowly crawl.
By the time he sees me, it's far too late.
My bloodied hand has sealed his fate.
As I plunge it into his chest, he gasps.
I have his heart within my grasp,
    no doubt cold from lack of use.
With one swift pull, I tear it loose.
He looks with shock as he hits the ground.
Now to me his ghost is bound.
The celestials granted me a final pleasure,
    a nexus where I'll torture his soul forever.

How does it feel to lose your skin?
No worse than the anguish I'll bring to him.

Acknowledgements

To
—my parents who have always been there for me and
—my brother Justin, who shares in my silliness and love for fiction
—my publisher Marcia, who gave me my first opportunity to have a book
—Jeff and Natalie Reynolds, the best bosses I've ever had and like second parents to me
—all my New Salem General Store work family, who have supported and encouraged me to pursue my dreams
Thank you all.

Alex Arnot

ABOUT THE POET

Alexander Arnot, better known as Alex, born August 6, 1996, has spent most of his life in Orange, Massachusetts.

Poetry and writing have always been a part of his life. As a child, he wrote lighthearted, silly poems in elementary school journals and while playing pretend with his friends. In his teens, he wrote dark, morbid song lyrics at home and in writing classes.

"The Dream Keeper" and other poems by Langston Hughes inspire his style and use of language. Media, literature, games, and music also inspire Alex to weave his thoughts and dreams into stories and poetry to share with the world and offer a look into his mind.

Alex enjoys science fiction, fantasy, and the supernatural with a later taste for horror. His journey to pursue poetry and writing began in his junior year of high school when he took his first creative writing class. A few years later, Alex joined a poetry website, poetfreak.com, where he shared his poems and met other poets. He also frequents and regularly posts to mypoeticside.com.

From the age of nineteen, Alex struggled with depression reflected in morbid and depressing poetry. From the age of twenty-four, he overcame depression and focuses on commentary and fantasy-based writing.

In his poetry, Alex attempts to craft worlds, characters, and stories in ways of a dream. He invites readers to join him on a journey through his thoughts, opinions, dreams, and nightmares.

COLOPHON

Type for poems in *Dreamscape Voyage* is set in Baskerville, a serif typeface designed in the 1750s by John Baskerville (1706–1775) in Birmingham, England, and cut into metal by punchcutter John Handy. Baskerville is classified as a transitional typeface, intended as a refinement of what are now called old-style typefaces of the period, especially those of his most eminent contemporary, William Caslon.

Titles are set in Copperplate Gothic. a typeface designed by Frederic W. Goudy and released by American Type Founders (ATF) in 1901. While termed a Gothic, another term for sans-serif, the face has small glyphic serifs that act to emphasize the blunt terminus of vertical and horizontal strokes. The typeface shows an unusual combination of influences. The glyphs are reminiscent of stone carving or lettering on copperplate engravings, and the wide horizontal axis is typical of Victorian display types.

www.ingramcontent.com/pod-product-compliance
Lightning Source LLC
Chambersburg PA
CBHW070649050426
42451CB00008B/320